Old Sarum A Handbook for Teachers Philippe Planel

Contents

Acknowledgements — Opposite
Introduction — 2
History of Old Sarum — 3
Preparing a Visit — 7
Preparing the Class — 8
Analysis of Units of Work — 10
Description of Units of Work — 11
Documents — 12

Units of Work — 17

Visiting Old Sarum — 27

Site Activity Sheets — 29
Follow up work — 34

Bibliography and Other Resources — 35
Site Plan — 36

Looking out from the East Gate

Old Sarum from the Amesbury Road

Introduction

Old Sarum is one of the most evocative sites in Southern England. Its windswept location, the juxtaposition of the stark earthworks with the shining spire of the 'new' city of Salisbury below, make a visit to Old Sarum a powerful experience for young and old.

Potential

The purpose of this handbook is to give Old Sarum some meaning for school children. All historical sites have interpretative strengths and weaknesses, limitations as well as potential. Whereas other sites in the custody of English Heritage, such as St Augustine's Abbey, Canterbury, or Portchester Castle are well suited to the study of architectural development through the ages, Old Sarum is not the best site for this purpose. Archaeologically Old Sarum also poses problems, since much of the site has not been excavated and there are consequently chronological gaps in the two millenia of its existence.

So why take children to Old Sarum? For certain purposes Old Sarum is an ideal site. The site has few rivals when it comes to examining continuity and discontinuity of settlement through a long timespan. The outline of the abandoned settlement, which responded to the needs of a succession of communities for over a thousand years, is still clearly visible. Even more visible is the new settlement of Salisbury in the valley below, offering a response to a different set of needs.

The reasons for a visit to Old Sarum, and the aims of this handbook are:

1. To situate a site in the landscape.

2. To situate a site in a timescape, and draw attention to important changes within that timescape.

3. To situate a site within a changing environment, and separate out human and natural agencies of environmental change.

4. To identify the processes of survival and destruction of standing remains.

5. To build an empathetic link with the past, relating a site to specific historical figures and events.

6. To demonstrate the full range of sources available to the student of the past.

The History of Old Sarum

Old Sarum lies on the chalk uplands 122 metres above sea level and about 73 metres above the river Avon. The site is about 3 kilometres north of the present city of Salisbury.

The site began life as an Iron Age hillfort of a type common in Wessex. Another Iron Age hillfort, Clearbury Ring, is visible from the ramparts of Old Sarum.

What distinguishes Old Sarum from many other Iron Age hillforts however is the use later communities were to put it to, namely the construction of a medieval castle, ecclesiastical buildings and cathedral within the perimeter of the Iron Age fortifications.

An aerial photograph of Old Sarum from the West

The Iron Age Hillfort

Immense effort was expended in the construction of the banks and ditches of Old Sarum. However, the builders were also able to make good use of the terrain to create this imposing earthwork choosing a spur of high ground reaching into the Avon valley. Old Sarum appears to be built on a separate hill, but this is only because the neck of land linking Old Sarum to the rest of the spur, Bishopsdown, was cut away to complete the defensive perimeter.

Archaeological excavations at Old Sarum have mainly been confined to the medieval elements within the original Iron Age perimeter. This means that we know very little about the Iron Age occupation of the site. There is little documentary evidence concerning the Iron Age in general and none at all for Old Sarum.

The Iron Age occupation of Old Sarum took place at some time between 500BC-50AD. It is not clear whether the site was a settlement in constant use or whether it only served to shelter a community and its livestock. Iron Age communities are seen by some archaeologists as practising an economy, and organising their society, on the ownership of cattle. Conflict might then have arisen from cattle stealing or arguments over pasturing. A hillfort must consequently have been spacious enough to shelter large herds of cattle. Old Sarum certainly contains a large enough area: 29.5 acres.

Old Sarum was probably a defensive site since the ditches are on the outside of the banks. The horn-work at the entrance to Old Sarum is also a purely defensive construction, restricting the impact of a concerted frontal attack.

Perhaps the single most important idea conveyed by the Iron Age fortifications is that of communal defence. The medieval builders at Old Sarum, whilst making use of the Iron Age ramparts, were ultimately concerned with protecting a small number of people in a restricted redoubt.

Horn work of the Iron Age hillfort

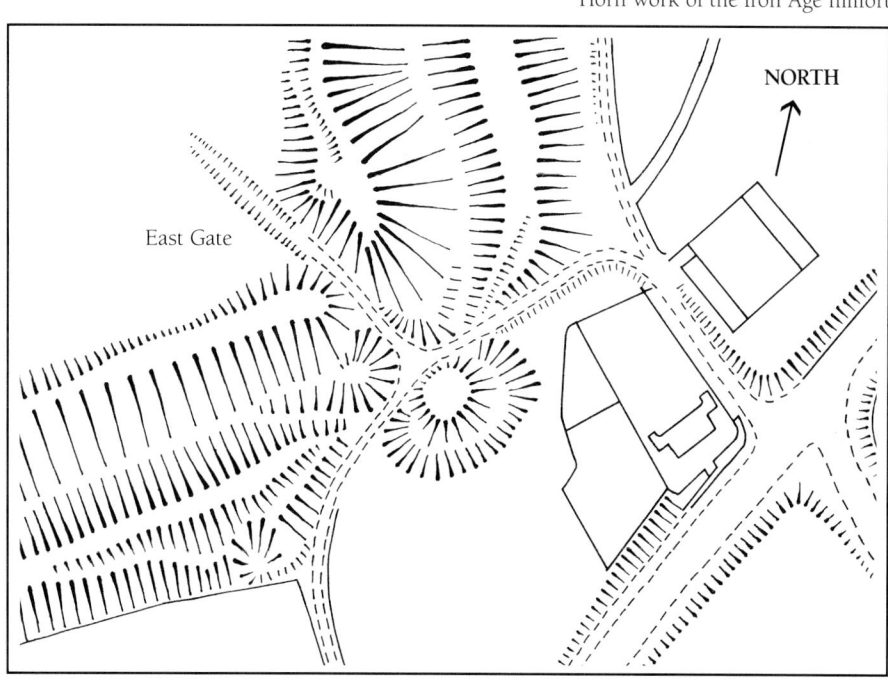

The History of Old Sarum

The Roman Period

Important Roman routes meet near Old Sarum (Sorviodunum): the roads from Winchester to Exeter, from Silchester and from the Severn via the Mendip hills. However despite this crossroads position, chance finds and limited excavation at Old Sarum do not indicate an intensive occupation of Old Sarum at this time, either by Romans or by the indigenous population and the Roman settlement was almost certainly not in the hillfort.

The Saxon Period

There are few indications that Old Sarum was in use during the early Saxon period although this period provides the first documentary reference to Old Sarum (see documents).

Saxon settlement in the Salisbury area, indicated principally by burial evidence, seems to have been confined to valley sites. It was probably only when defence once again became a preoccupation that Old Sarum was resettled. Viking raids became endemic from the ninth century onwards, and by the eleventh century nowhere in Wessex was safe. Saxon artefacts from this period have been found at Old Sarum and from 1004, shortly after Wilton was overrun by the Danish king Sweyn, Old Sarum is known to have operated a mint. These coins bear the name 'Serebrig'. There is also some archaeological evidence to suggest that the defences of Old Sarum were strengthened at this time. There are however only minor domestic finds from what may have been a burgeoning Late Saxon centre. Several centuries of unbroken settlement follow at Old Sarum.

The Normans and the Medieval Period

It is with the Norman Conquest, over a thousand years after the original Iron Age occupation of Old Sarum that important additions and modifications were made to the site.

The Norman Motte at Old Sarum

The Normans' first step was to build an inner stronghold within the existing perimeter. The first Norman castle, or 'motte' was probably built out of wood on a raised platform of earth and converted to stone as soon as time permitted. The choice of an existing defensive system was common Norman practice as this saved the trouble of building an outer bailey. The same was done at Portchester Castle, where the Norman castle is built within a Roman shore fort.

The eastern part of the Iron Age hillfort became the outer bailey, and banks and ditches running south and north-east from the motte further defined this area (see plan in unit 3).

This left the western part of the hillfort free for non-military use and permitted the construction of a western entrance into the complex.

In 1092 a cathedral was consecrated in the north-west quadrant of the site by Bishop Osmund. It was entirely in keeping with the long-term policy of 'conquest' that Norman bishops in Norman cathedrals should replace the scattered rural Saxon bishoprics and that this spiritual authority should exist in close proximity with Norman civil and military power. Bishop Roger (1107-1139) was by no means unusual in combining the roles of civil, military and religious authority in one person, and the bishop's palace was also his castle. (Bishop Roger's secular interests brought about his downfall in the civil war of the mid 12th century.)

It was only later in the century that the bishop came to occupy a palace near the cathedral, outside the inner bailey. It was this separation of religious and military powers that led to the tensions which eventually brought about the foundation of the existing cathedral in Salisbury and the abandonment of Old Sarum.

The first cathedral burnt down only five days after its consecration in 1092. This early cathedral, with its apsidal east end and transeptal towers of Frankish influence, was replaced by one with a central tower, reflecting Bishop Roger's Norman origin.

A Gold coin minted at Old Sarum, bearing the head of Ethelred the Unready (978-1016), and the name 'Serebrig' on the reverse side

English Heritage

The History of Old Sarum

However by the time the cathedral was being built Old Sarum must have already been a place of national importance, as it was chosen by William as the meeting point for the great Oath of Allegiance of 1085.

Other buildings of a humbler nature were built at Old Sarum. There is little doubt that a new town was developing. Until recently it had been assumed that the town was in the outer bailey but evidence now suggests it was outside the defences. Unlike the communal defence of the Iron Age the Normans did not regard it as their concern to defend a civilian population, indeed they were prepared to face the eventuality of defending themselves from the civilian population.

By the 13th century it was clear that the arrangements at Old Sarum were not to everyone's liking, a fact well illustrated by a poem of the period (see documents). As far as the church was concerned, matters came to a head in 1217 when the Dean and clergy of Old Sarum, not being allowed keys to the outer gate, found themselves locked out on their return from a rogationtide procession.

However the civilian population may have already decided to move away from Old Sarum in some numbers, and there is a reference to dwindling congregations at Old Sarum at this time. The early 13th century was marked by widespread pressure for the creation of new towns. This pressure was exerted by ordinary people as much as by lay and ecclesiastical landlords, the latter seeing towns and the revenue they generated as a useful source of income.

At Old Sarum the church and a growing community of merchants may well have found common cause in moving to a more congenial site in the valley below. Defence was not as important a criterion in choosing a site for a settlement as it had been. This left the military alone above the new town, and with the end of the medieval period and the end of medieval military trappings, Old Sarum once again found itself without a role, except as a quarry for building stone.

An aerial photograph of Old Sarum from the West

A general view of excavations at Old Sarum c.1910

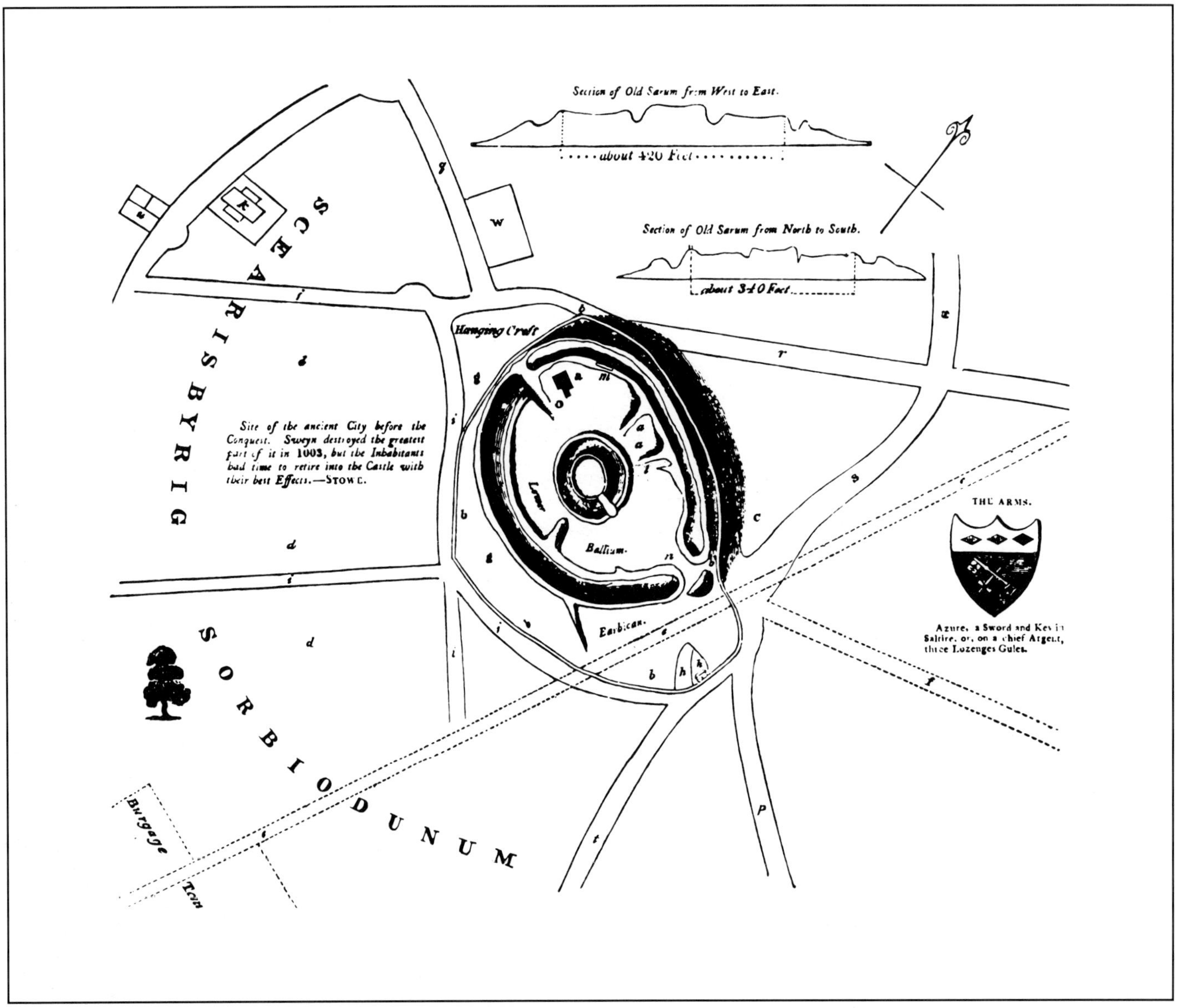

The History of Old Sarum

A map of Old Sarum, drawn by Henry Wansey and published in 1819

Old Sarum in Our Era

Antiquarian interest in Old Sarum began as early as 1540 with Leland's visit to the area. The overgrown ruins acquired a certain amount of notoriety in the 18th century as a 'rotten borough' and in the following century a map of the area was produced showing the main features of the site. Two small excavations were carried out before more serious attempts in 1909; these explored the underground passage, discovered in 1795, and the foundations of the cathedral (1834). Since 1892 Old Sarum has been in the custody of the State.

The 1909-15 excavations were by the standards of the time a very rigorous operation, carried out with military precision by a military man, Lt Col Hawley. The excavation reports and photographs tell us almost as much about Edwardian times as they do about Old Sarum's past.

In the present decade the importance of Old Sarum and even the landscape around the site have been recognised by the city planners and the public at large to be of considerable cultural significance. One of the proposed Salisbury by-pass routes which would have run below the northern ramparts was opposed because of this interest.

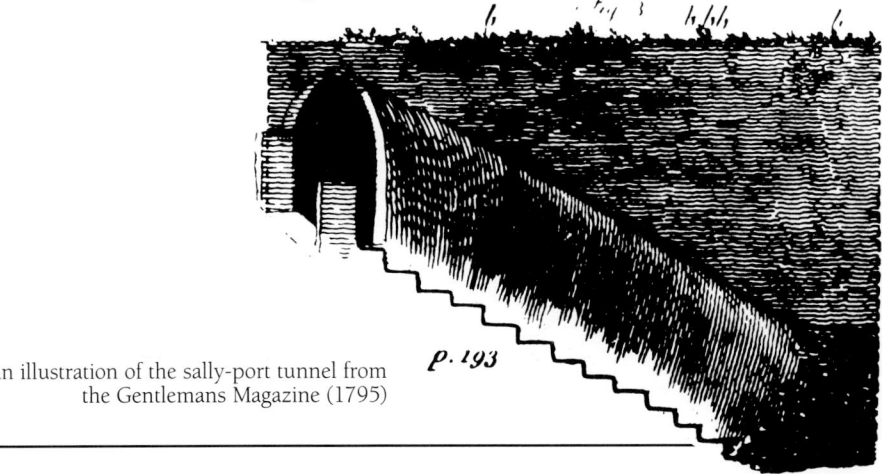

An illustration of the sally-port tunnel from the Gentlemans Magazine (1795)

Preparing a visit to Old Sarum

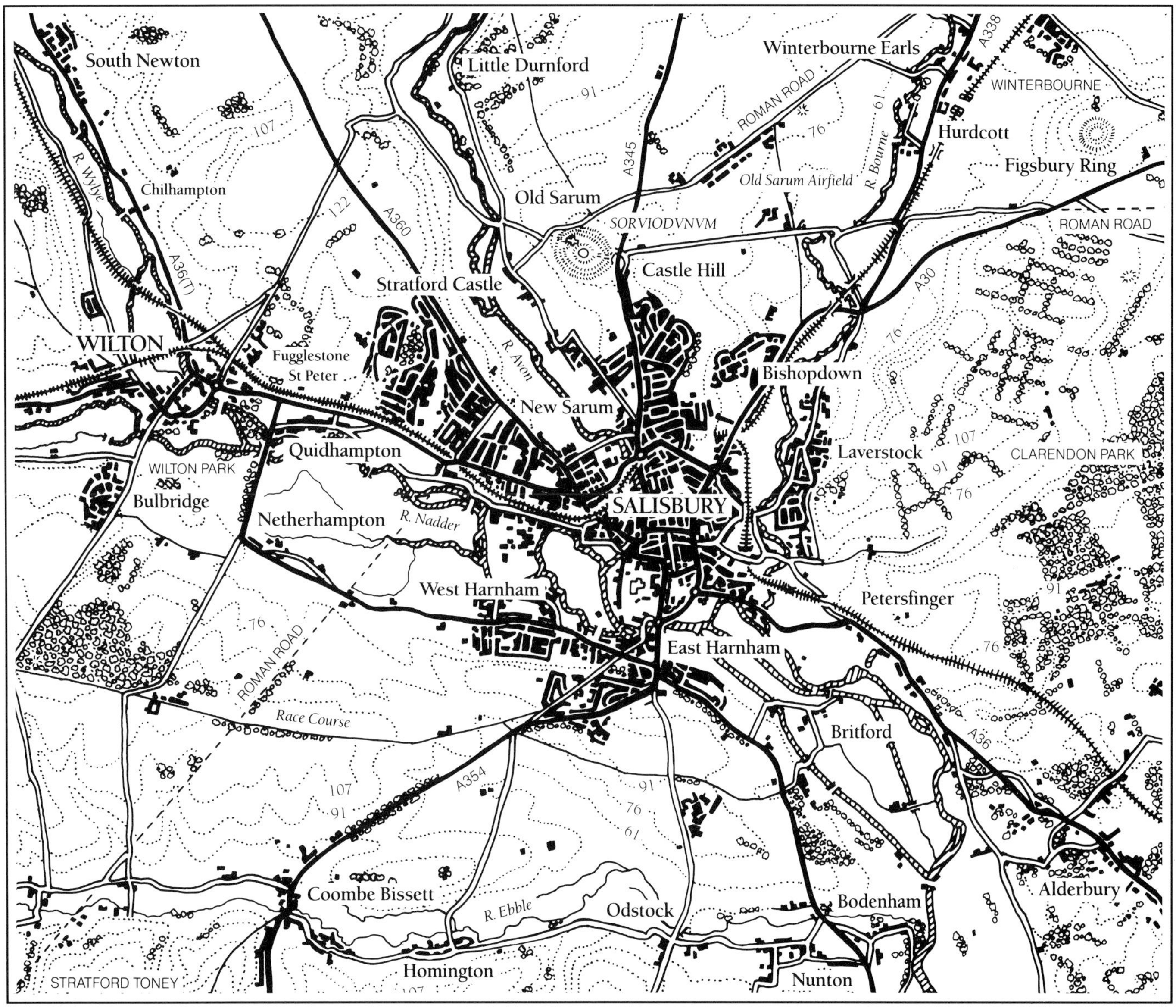

A location map of Old Sarum and the Salisbury area

How to Book

Write to:

English Heritage
South West Area Office
Bridge House
Sion Place
Clifton
Bristol BS8 4XA
Tel: Bristol (0272) 734472

There is no charge for pre-booked school visits. There is a free planning visit for teachers.

Parking

Good for coaches with proviso that coaches cannot turn into Old Sarum approaching from Salisbury, the turn is too tight. If there is time the coach can drop children in the layby opposite the Old Castle pub. Walking through the Iron Age defences gives children a better introduction to the site. The coach can then turn and pick children up from the car park.

Facilities

There is plenty of room for picnicking at Old Sarum, but it is an exposed site and can be very windy. Public lavatories are available in the bailey car park.

Associated Sites

Salisbury Museum

The finds from Old Sarum can be seen at the museum, in particular the small finds from the garderobe pits (see Unit 9). The museum is within the cathedral close and is free for Wiltshire schools. There is a small charge for parties from other counties. Preliminary visits by teachers are free of charge. The museum offers a study-room in the winter months which may, by prior arrangement, also be used to eat packed lunches.

Address:

The King's House
65 The Close
Salisbury
Wiltshire SP1 2EN
Telephone: Salisbury (0722) 332151

Preparing a visit to Old Sarum

Salisbury Cathedral

The cathedral is very close to the museum and it is a good way to end the day to look at the 'new' cathedral, since the building of this cathedral was one of the determining factors in the move from Old Sarum. The effigies of three Old Sarum bishops, Osmund, Roger and Jocelin, are in the cathedral. It is possible to split the day between Old Sarum, the cathedral and museum, and not exhaust the children.

Coaches for the Cathedral Close usually park beside the East wall of the close in Exeter Street. Teachers can point out the decorated stones in the East wall that were reused from Old Sarum.

Address:

Visitors Education Officer
Chapter Office
6 The Close
Salisbury
Wiltshire
Tel: Salisbury (0722) 28726

School parties to the cathedral should be booked in at least a week in advance. The cathedral has a small contribution for each child. Free guides are available and a visit to the cathedral workshops can be arranged. This visit is to be especially recommended, since classes will be able to see stone being worked, a technique that has hardly changed in a thousand years.

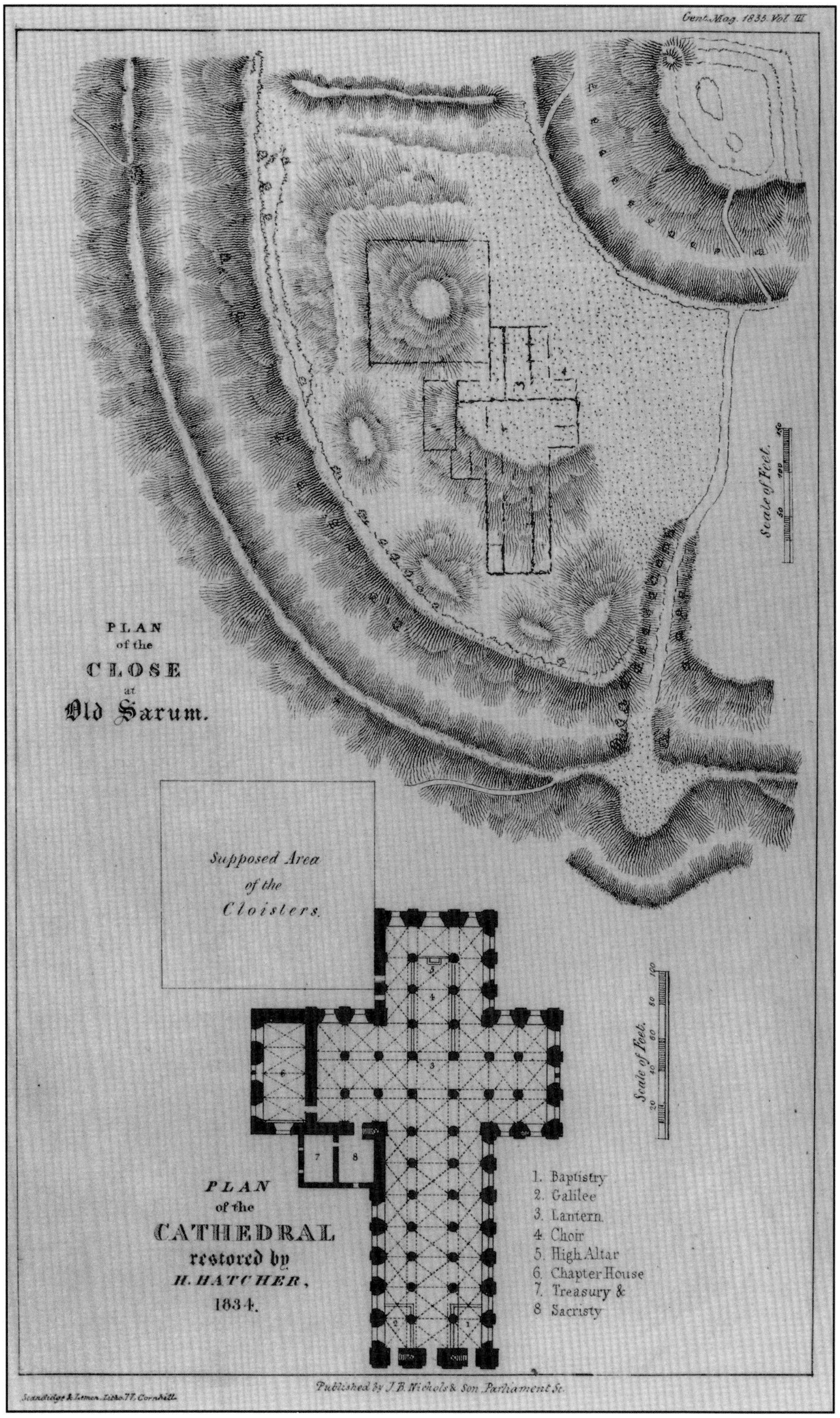

Preparing the Class

1. Any work on settlement choice and settlement location is very useful, as are all mapping and planning skills.

2. Knowledge of the chronology of the Iron Age, Roman, Saxon, Norman and Medieval periods and also of churches, cathedrals, monasteries, castles is not assumed, but again, will be of great advantage.

3. The units of work give detailed preparation for the visit to Old Sarum, and these should be completed before the visit.

4. Teachers might wish to consider the project within a general discussion of how we value our heritage. Once raised children usually have clear views on this subject, and the subject can lead to cross-curricular work.

Most buildings that have stood the test of time are the better constructed buildings of the wealthy. Where is the heritage of the labouring poor that have always constituted the backbone of our society?

Plan of the close at Old Sarum, 1834

The Units of Work

Content

It is intended that the material in this booklet will be useful for history teachers and teachers running integrated humanities courses.

Old Sarum is situated in a landscape

Preparing a visit to Old Sarum

which is still evolving and the handbook gives consideration to development proposals near the site and the concern to protect it. There is an important and 'living' relationship between sites and their landscapes. Some teachers might wish to consider an even wider brief and take in other important medieval sites around Salisbury, the Laverstock potteries and Clarendon Palace for example, setting them within the historical and archaeological landscape.

The classwork in this booklet is not of a uniform level and teachers are best placed to determine the elements most suited to their classes. Broadly speaking the units are intended for the 9-14 age range.

The Units

1. Choosing the right place to live

2. Old Sarum in the Iron Age

3. The Normans at Old Sarum

4. A bit of history

5. Problems between Castle and Cathedral

6. What happened to Old Sarum?

7. Old Sarum under the spade and trowel (1909-1915)

8. To excavate or not to excavate?

9. The garderobe pits

10. Old Sarum and the modern landscape.

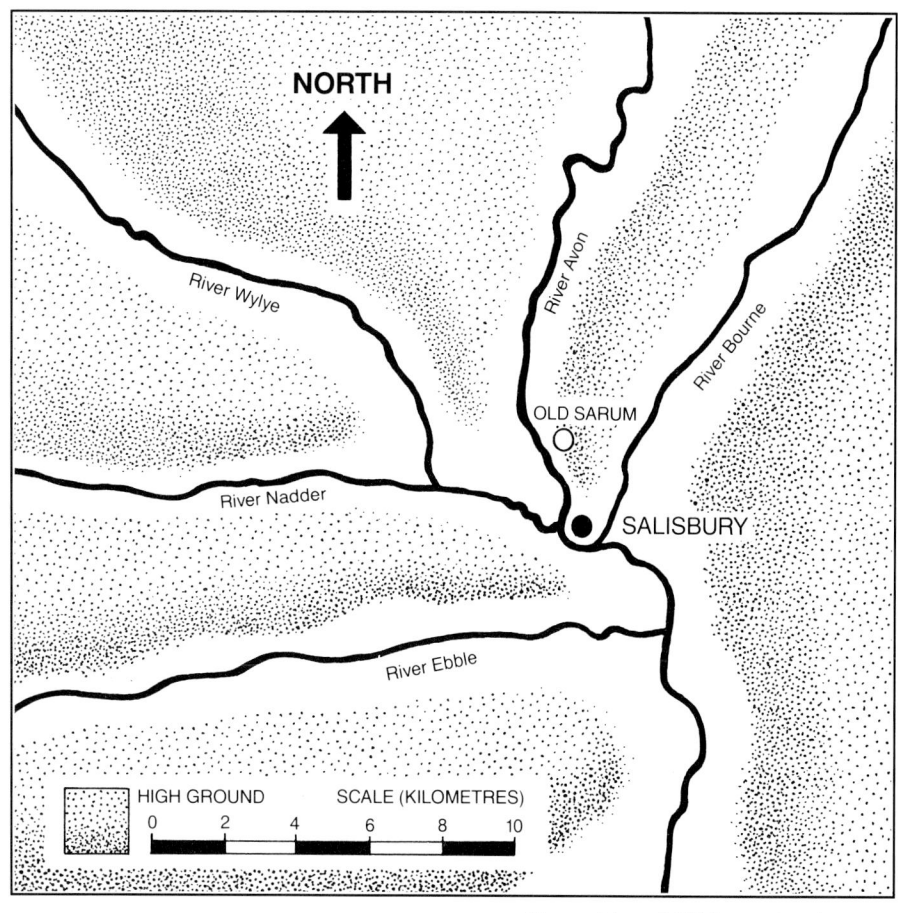

The position of Old Sarum in relation to local rivers

An engraving of Old Sarum from the East

Analysis of Units of Work

Unit No.	Key ideas	Skills involved	Content	Activities	Extra Resources
1	Settlement	Map making	Map of Avon valley	Drawing hand	The human hand
2	How we represent features on the ground	Drawing and interpretation	Scale Plans Hachures Sections	Tadpole exercise	Background on Iron Age
3	Evaluating evidence	Selecting ideas	Norman choice of Old Sarum	Multiple choice exercise	Background on Normans
4	Chronology	Sequencing events	Old Sarum Time chart	Completing table Questions	
5	Historical empathy	Interpreting primary sources Empathy	Castle and cathedral in conflict	Questions	Documents as source material
6	Evaluating evidence	Interpreting primary sources	Old Sarum replaced by Salisbury	Questions, filling-in blanks	Documents as source material
7	Analysing evidence	Using excavation report	Evidence of 1909-1915 excavation	Questions	Archaeologist's Report
8	Views of the past	Balancing conflicting views	Environmental criticism of excavations	Group work debate	
9	Evaluating evidence Empathy	Using excavation reports	Detailed small find report	Questions	
10	The past, the future	Planning for conservation	A36 proposed by-pass	Preparation of report	

Description of Units of Work

The Units of Work

1. The first unit owes a debt to W H Hudson and his introduction to *'A Shepherd's Life'*. Hudson hit on the idea of representing the five tributaries of the river Avon by the five fingers of the hand. This quickly establishes the parameters imposed by the landscape on human settlement in the area.

2. Apart from describing the site of Old Sarum, the second unit attempts to involve children in finding a symbolic language to express, on paper, features on the ground. The tadpole exercise should equip children to deal with the plans of Old Sarum.

3. and 4. These two units of work are very straightforward exercises to demonstrate the Norman implantation of Old Sarum and the historical importance of the site.

5. Contemporary 13th century documents show that, for at least one section of the population, Old Sarum had ceased to fulfil its usefulness, and support the argument that the site really was a bleak place to live. Complaints about being 'blinded by the chalk' give a useful insight into how different the site was then, when most of the earthworks — since they were cut into the chalk — would have presented a vision of a white hill-top. The grass probably grew back only in later centuries.

6. Old Sarum as a quarry. The gradual desertion of the site is again chronicled by surviving documents.

7. We now move forward nearly 500 years to the first, and to this date, the only, systematic excavation of the site. During these 500 years little occurred at Old Sarum, besides a gradual grassing over of the ruins. A detailed consideration of the finds is left until later, for the moment it is the method and means of excavation that are considered.

8. Hudson's help is again enlisted in this unit to show that it is not only recently that there have been conflicting views on what is now called 'cultural resource management'. In the documents section a letter from General Pitt-Rivers also demonstrates the importance attached to Old Sarum from the late 19th century onwards.

9. A detailed examination of the small finds from the 1909-1915 excavations at Old Sarum and the light they throw on life there in Norman times. Larger finds, i.e. buildings, form the basis of the visit to the site and are not treated in these units.

10. The storm over the A36 by-pass will soon be history, but at the time of writing this handbook it is a controversial issue, not the least controversial element being the proposed 'Route C' passing below the ramparts of Old Sarum.

Excavation of the East gate, 1909

Documents

Anglo-Saxon Chronicle 552AD

The first clear reference to Old Sarum. As yet there is no corroborative evidence for occupation at this time.

"In this year Cynric fought against the Britons at the place called Searoburh, and put the Britons to flight."

Poem of the early 13th century

Written by Henry D'Avranches on the removal of Salisbury cathedral, translated from the Latin by Robin Torrance in the Wiltshire Archaeological Magazine, 1956.

"I propose to explain why Bishop Richard moved Salisbury cathedral. Sarum Hill was in many ways like Mount Gilboa. It was covered with neither grass nor flowers. It was sodden with rain and dew. Nothing beautiful nor useful could grow there, nothing except wormwood: and a tree is known by its fruit.

A fortress stands upon a hill, exposed only to the winds, which were strong enough to shake its summit. Little water was to be found; but chalk in abundance. The winds howled, but no nightingale ever sang. The chalk soil was bad enough, but the shortage of water even worse. The former dazzled the eyes, and the latter provoked thirst. The silence of birds was a loss still worse than the violence of the wind. The one deprived us of pleasure, and the other deprived us of our very dwellings.

Against their will they (the clergy) had to supply uninvited soldiers with food, and, what was worse, even the poor had to leave their homes of refuge, lest they be driven away in disgrace.

So now we can see how much harm shortage of water can do. Nothing can be worse for the inhabitants of a city. Water quenches thirst and extinguishes fires. Boats and ships float upon water, carrying a wealth of merchandise. It washes away dirt and stains. It gives life to grass and flowers, and new life to birds and little fish... What then will be the state of a city which lacks water for its people?... There can be no greater evil for a city than drought.

The steep ascent to the city was tiring, whether going up or down. It was slippery and dangerous. In going up the chest hurts through shortness of breath, in coming down the foot may slip."

Papal Bull, 1219

Papal authority was required for the removal of the cathedral to a new site. The grounds for removal are summarised in this Bull of Pope Honorius III.

"Situated within a castle, the church is subject to such inconvenience that the clergy cannot stay there without danger to their persons. The church is exposed to such winds that those celebrating the divine offices can hardly hear each other speak. The fabric is so ruinous that it is a constant danger to the congregation which has dwindled to the extent that it is hardly able to provide for the repair of the roofs, which are constantly damaged by the winds. Water is so scarce that it has to be bought at a high price, and access to it is not to be had without the governor's permission. People wishing to enter the cathedral are often prevented by guards from the garrison. Housing is insufficient for the clergy who are therefore forced to buy houses from laymen. The whiteness of the chalk causes blindness."

Documents

Calendar of Patent Rolls, 1331

Documentary evidence corroborating the evidence from the markings on the stones in the wall of the present cathedral close, as to the reuse of stone from Old Sarum in the new cathedral and town. This evidence also confirms that the cathedral at Old Sarum was no longer in use.

"March 1st, Croydon.

Gift to R. Bishop of Salisbury, and to the Dean and Chapter of the church of St Mary, Salisbury, of the stones of the old cathedral church at Old Sarum and of the houses within the King's castle there which the Bishop and Canons of that church formerly occupied, for the repair of their church and for the enclosure of the precinct thereof."

Calendar of Patent Rolls, 1336

Old Sarum was to continue in use as a prison, but even this was not well maintained and the following commission follows a mass breakout and the murder of a sheriff's clerk in 1336. The last recorded gaol delivery at Old Sarum is in 1414.

"March 16th, Westminster.

Commission to Peter Eskydemour and Richard De Penlye, to survey the castle of Old Sarum, where, as is reported, the King's prison is in so ruinous a state that it feared that the prisoners will escape, and many other defects exist; and to find by jury of the county of Wilts by whose neglect it has fallen into decay and all other particulars."

Letter and Papers of Henry VIII, 1514

This establishes the abandonment of Old Sarum by 1514, with another grant for the removal of building stone.

"29. Thomas Compton, groom of the chamber. Grant of the stone walls and stones called the castle or tower of Old Sarum, Wilts, with liberty to knock down and carry away the said walls . . .(with preliminary petition which states the castle is standing beside New Sarum in a desolate and barren place and can never be inhabitable)."

John Leland's Itinerary (1540), p 260

John Leland is one of England's earliest antiquaries, and some of his comments furnish us with historical and topographical detail not available from other sources.

"The site of Old-Saresbyri standing on a hille is distant from the new a mile by north weste, and is in cumpace half a mile and more.

This thing hath beene auncient and exceding strong: but syns the building of New-Saresbyri it went totally to ruine.

Sum think that lak of water caussid the inhabitantes to relinquisch the place; yet were ther many welles or swete water.

Sum say, that after that in tyme of civile warres that castelles and waullid townes wer kept that the castellanes Old-Saresbyri and the chanons could not agre, insomuch that the castellanes apon a tyme prohibited them cumming home from Procession and Rogation to re-entre the town. Wherapon the bisshop and they consulting togither at the last began a chirch on their own propre soyle: and then the people resortid straight to New-Saresbyri and buildid ther: and then in continuaunce were a great numbre of the houses of Old-Saresbyri pullid doun and set up at New-Saresbyri.

Osmund Erle of Dorchestre and after Bisshop of Saresbyri erectid his cathedrale chirch ther in the west part of the town: and also his palace. Whereof now no token is but only a chapelle or our Lady yet stanisnf and mainteynid.

Documents

John Leland's Itinerary Cont.

Ther was a paroch of the Holy Rode beside in Old-Saresbyri: and an other over the est gate wherof yet sum tokens remayne.

I do not perceyve that ther were any mo gates in Old-Saresbyri then 2, one by est, and an other by west. Withoute eche of these gates was a fair suburnbe. And yn the est suburbe was a paroch chirch of S John: and ther yet is a chapelle standinge.

The ryver is a good quarter of a mile from Old-Saresbyri and more where it is nerest onto it, and that is Stratford village, south from it.

Ther hath beene houses in tyme of mynd inhabitid in the est suburbe of Old-Saresbyri: but now ther is not one house nother within Old-Saresbyri or without inhabited.

Ther was a right fair and strong castelle within Old-Saresbyri longging to the Erles of Saresbyri especially the Longespees.
I read that one Gualterus was the first Erle after the conquest of it.

Much notable ruinus building of this castelle yet ther remaynith. The diche that environid the old toun was a very deepe and strong thynge."

General Pitt-Rivers

General Pitt-Rivers was one of the foremost archaeologists of the 19th century and lived on nearby Cranbourne Chase. One of Pitt-Rivers' letters, dated July 3 1891, reveals that he was contemplating purchasing and excavating Old Sarum. The letter also reveals the "enlightened despotism" which was the hall-mark of many of the great Victorian archaeologists.

"The editor of the Salisbury Times wrote to me a short time ago to ask my object in proposing to purchase Old Sarum, and I told him in a letter, not for publication, that, if I made the purchase, it would be for the purpose of archaeological explorations, and also to make it more attractive to those who took an interest in the place. I think it only requires a little common sense to show that no-one would be likely to make such an unprofitable investment, except for some purpose of that kind. I see that Mr Waters, in a letter to one of the papers, says that he does not think that the prosecution of archaeological explorations would be consistent with the rights of the citizen. I don't know what the rights of the citizen may be or how it would be likely to interfere with them, but if that is the case, of course I should give up all idea of making the purchase.

It is evident from what has been said, that in order to carry on excavations satisfactorily it would be quite necessary that I should maintain existing rights of ownership intact; and that with people constantly meddling and asserting themselves on every opportunity, the investigations would be greatly interfered with."

General Pitt-Rivers

Salisbury and South Wiltshire Museum

Documents

W H Hudson (1910)

W H Hudson was a noted Wiltshire naturalist and writer. His views about Old Sarum can best be seen as a hangover from the 19th century view on romantic ruins. From 'A Shepherd's Life', p 22.

"Nature had made it a sweet and beautiful spot; the earth over the old buried ruins was covered with an elastic turf, jewelled with the bright little flowers of the chalk . . .

Once only during the last five or six centuries some slight excavations were made when, in 1834, as a result of an excessively dry summer, the lines of the cathedral foundations were discernible on the surface. But it will no longer be the place it was, the Society of Antiquaries having received permission from the Dean and Chapter of Salisbury to work their sweet will on the site. That ancient beautiful carcass, which had long made their mouths water, on which they have now fallen like a pack of hungry hyenas to tear off the old hide of green turf and burrow down to open to the light or drag out the deep, stony framework. The beautiful surrounding thickets, too, must go, they tell me, since you cannot turn the hill inside out without destroying the trees and bushes that crown it."

Excavation of the chapel

Documents

Archaeologist's Report

An abridged description of various items recovered during excavations at Old Sarum.
Specific Location of finds listed: The Garderobe Pits of the Keep   (1910-1915 Seasons)

No.	Item/s found	Description of article or remains thereof:
1	Pots	Several hundredweights of sherds (pieces of pottery) were found. These were mainly the remains of discarded cooking pots and jugs. Some of these pieces have "... *pretty designs upon them chiefly floral, and others have those of weird animals*".
2	Glass	Many fragments of glass were unearthed as well. Some of these were from overseas — including some from Venice. Much of the glass was very ornately patterned: "*There had been vessels, seemingly decanters and cups, of a beautiful dark blue glass, often with a ribbed outside pattern, and one piece has gold burnt upon it*".
3	Lace	"*The most interesting find is a piece of lace, formed of gold thread woven into silk, and it is marvellous how it escaped destruction*".
4	Iron	"*Of iron there are keys, knife blades, heads of hammers and other tools, padlocks, side licks, buckles, scissors shaped like shears, ankle manacles and a window bar .. and many other small articles*".
5	Bronze, Copper and Brass	"*There are hawks' bells of brass, round-headed pins of the same metal, and a small needle; part of a bronze spur*".
6	Lead	"*... a few pieces of rectangular window frames .. what would appear to be a lead pencil*".
7	Shaped Bone	"*There is a flageolet (wind instrument) made of the ulna of a swan's wing ... bone rings ... two ladies' corsets or busk bones ... two draughtsmen ...*"
8	Bone	Many animal bones were discovered. For example, the remains of "*... fallow deer .. antlers of fallow deer, roe deer ... sheep, ox, pig, duck, and common fowl, some with well developed spurs which indicate cock-fighting. Bones of partridge, snipe and many kinds of small birds also occurred*".
9	Shells and Fish	"*There were large quantities of oyster shells; also the shells of mussel, whelk, cockle and winkle, and the broken claws of crabs. Bones of fish and patches of their scales were often found, though it is not clear what fish they were; but sea fish were certainly present, as the bones of flat fish were discovered. Bodies of dogs, cats and rodents found a last resting place in the pits, and their bones add variety to the list*".
10	Gold	A gold ring was found.

Unit 1. Choosing the right place to live

Follow these instructions carefully:

1 Spread out your right hand on the page and draw round it with a pencil.

2 Now lightly shade the area outside the shape of your hand, choosing a colour that you think is suitable for high land or hills.

The space left where your hand was represents a large river valley with five smaller valleys joining it.

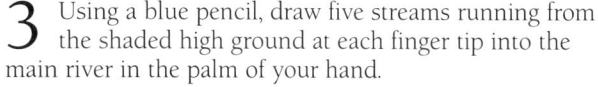

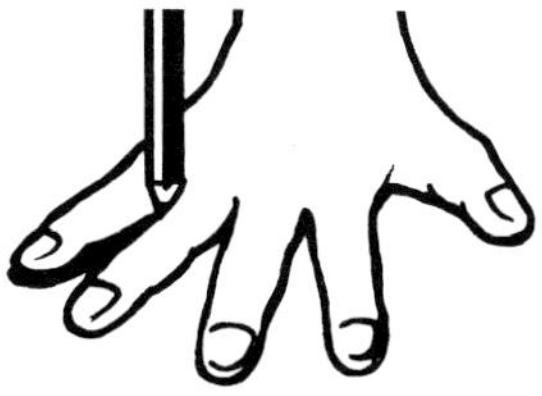

3 Using a blue pencil, draw five streams running from the shaded high ground at each finger tip into the main river in the palm of your hand.

4 Study the map you have drawn and decide on the best location for two settlements:

Settlement (a) would be where you could control the area and protect yourself from attack.

Settlement (b) would be where you could have a running water supply to clean the street and where there was no need for defence.

Mark (a) with a cross and (b) with a small circle.

In fact you have drawn a map of the Avon valley in Wiltshire. If you compare it with the real map that your teacher will show you, you will be able to see whether you chose the same sort of place to put your settlements as the people of Old Sarum and Salisbury did in real life hundreds of years ago.

Old Sarum

Unit 2. Old Sarum in the Iron Age

About 2000 years ago, in the Iron Age a series of banks and ditches were dug at Old Sarum; they are still there today.

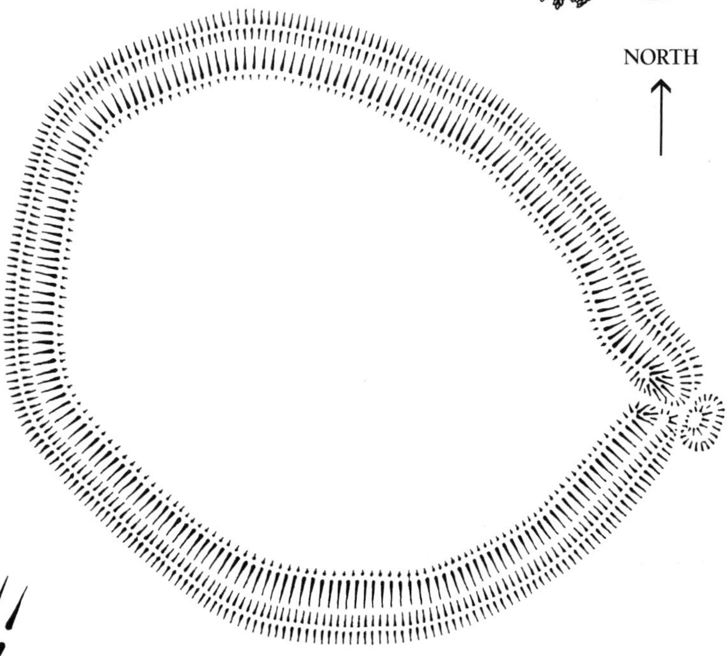

NORTH ↑

1. Draw a centimetre square in the middle of the plan. This is about the size of a football pitch.

The plan is drawn in such a way that you can tell which way the ground slopes and work out where the banks and ditches are. If you look closely at the lines used in the plan you will see that each line looks a bit like a tadpole: the lines are thicker at one end than they are at the other.

All you have to remember is that the thick end of each line always faces in the direction of higher ground, so where the thick ends meet we have the top of a bank, like this:

2. What do you think is represented by this:

Answer:

3. Draw a plan of your school with a bank and ditch around it, with the bank on the inside.

4. Imagine that you are on the inside, trying to stop people from the outside getting in. Is it better for you to be on the bank on the inside, on a higher position? Or would it be better for you if the attacker was on the bank opposite you? Think about these problems and then try to answer the question.

Answer:

5. Although the view from above (plan view) tells us a good deal, we may want to see what a bank and ditch, for example, looks like from the side. Archaeologists call this a *section*. Here is a section showing what the bank and ditch at Old Sarum look like today and as it probably looked in the Iron Age, (the dotted line). What differences do you notice?

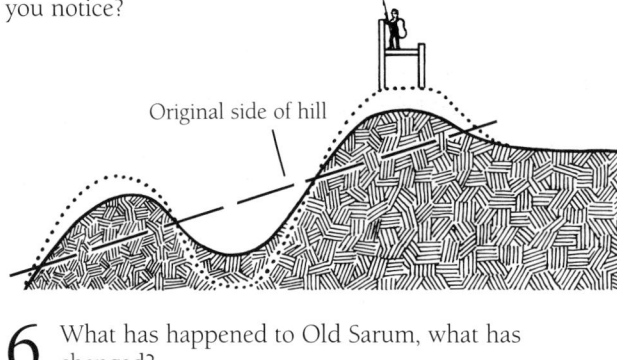

Original side of hill

6. What has happened to Old Sarum, what has changed?

Answer:

18 Old Sarum

Name: .... Class: ....

Unit 3. The Normans at Old Sarum

The next major building stage at Old Sarum took place at least a thousand years after the first bank and ditch were built. After the Norman invasion in 1066 the Normans were anxious to protect themselves from the Anglo-Saxons, the native population.

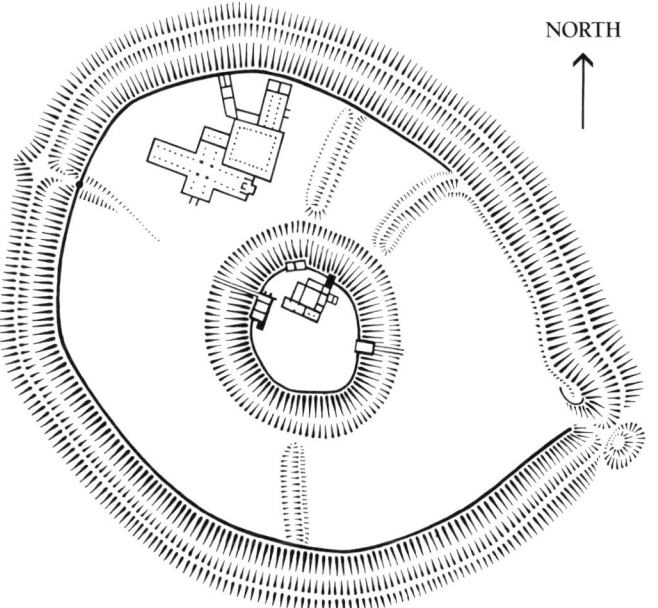

NORTH

1. Why do you think the Normans built a castle in the middle of Old Sarum?

   a. Because they wanted a good view
   b. Because it saved them work to build in the middle of an old hillfort
   c. Because they wanted to be out of the way if the Avon flooded
   d. Because it was a pretty place

   Answer:

2. Why do you think the Normans tended to build in wood at first and convert to stone later?

   a. Because they suddenly realised that wood rots
   b. Because they had to burn the wood to keep warm in winter
   c. Because they had to choose what was quickest until they were safe
   d. Because they built in wood in Normandy and were not allowed to change castle plans at first

   Answer:

3. Why do you think the Normans built a cathedral so close to the castle?

   a. Because they wanted control over all important things, including the church
   b. Because they needed to be close to go and pray in the night
   c. Because they had so much spare stone when they had finished the castle
   d. Because it was supposed to give good luck to built a cathedral in an old hillfort

   Answer:

A Norman 'motte and bailey' castle. The motte is the earth bank. The bailey is the outer defence. The first castle at Old Sarum may have looked like this, using the Iron Age bank and ditch as the outer bailey. Later on the stone castle was itself set on a bigger mound inside its own 'inner bailey', making a total of three lines of defence.

Old Sarum

Unit 4. A bit of history

Old Sarum was an important place in the Norman period. Important meetings were held there as it was a secure place. It was also a central place for the great lords of Southern England and a place not far from the coast, and the French lands that belonged to the English kings at this time.

Time Chart

Look at the time chart and then:

1 Enter your date of birth at the right place in the chart and then write "I was born" next to it.

2 Something on the chart tells us the Saxon name for Old Sarum
  a. Where is this shown?

Answer:

  b. What is the name?

Answer:

3 Shade the main periods in different colours: Iron Age, Roman, Saxon, Norman, Medieval, 1500AD to the present — find your own name for this last period. In real life these periods blended into each other, so try and show this in your colouring.

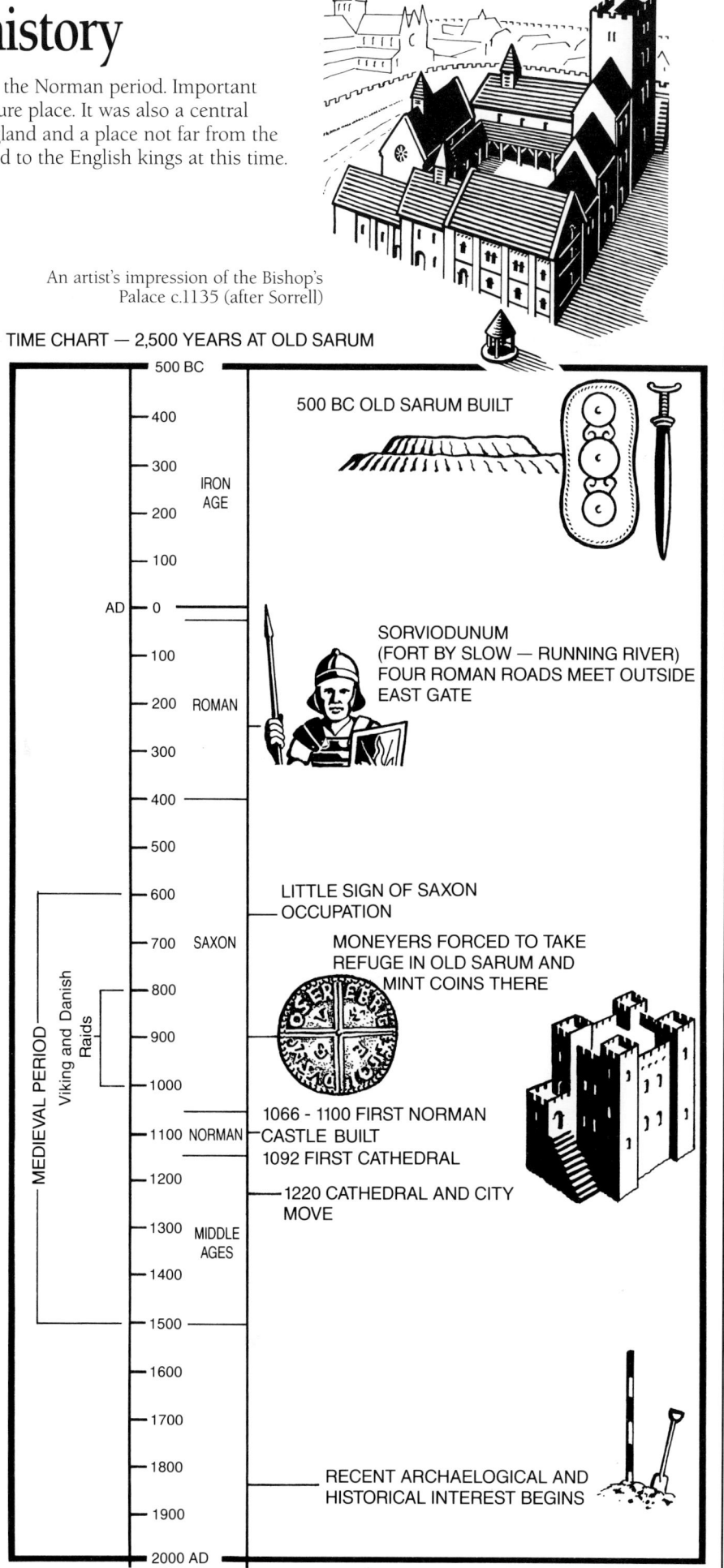

An artist's impression of the Bishop's Palace c.1135 (after Sorrell)

20   Old Sarum

Unit 5. Problems between Castle and Cathedral

An artist's impression of Bishop Roger's Cathedral c.1130 (after Sorrell)

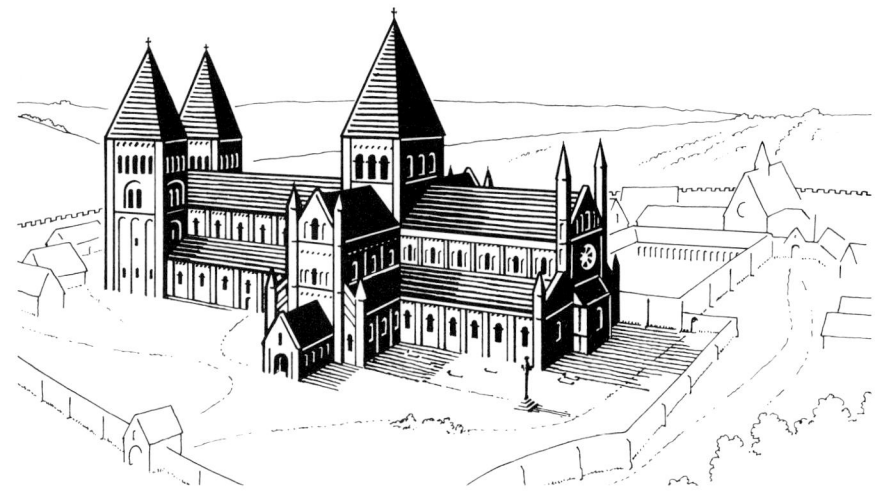

Bishop Roger from an effigy in Salisbury Cathedral

It was the 12th century bishop, Roger, who was the most active builder at Old Sarum. He got permission from the king to rebuild the castle and he also built a new cathedral. People at the time said that the cathedral was so good, it looked as if it had been built from a single stone.

Until the mid 12th century the Norman mound at the centre of Old Sarum had contained the bishop's palace as well as the castle. But after 1142, the bishop built a palace near the cathedral, that is, in the outer bailey. Tension mounted later in the century as the bishop found he could only enter Old Sarum with the permission of the soldiers in the castle.

Source A: Papal Bull of Pope Honorius III, (1219)

1 What was Bishop Richard Poore complaining about? Make a list of the complaints, in what you think was their order of importance.

Answer:

2 Do you think people may already have been moving out of Old Sarum at this stage? Why? Is there any evidence for what you think?

Answer:

Source B: Poem of the early 13th century

1 What further problems does this poem complain about?

Answer:

2 There is another reference to chalk 'dazzling' people here, what can this mean?

Answer:

3 Why would a new city and cathedral down in the river valley be more agreeable? Would they have any disadvantages?

Answer:

Old Sarum

Unit 6. What happened to Old Sarum?

Work began on the new cathedral in the valley below about 1220, and Old Sarum's days were numbered. The townsfolk had probably already begun to move down to Salisbury. Once the church and congregation began to desert the hill top, this only left the Sheriff and soldiers. For some time the castle was maintained and parts of it were even rebuilt. Then the whole site fell into disuse.

Look at the three source documents:

Source A: Calendar of Patent Rolls, 1331.

Source B: Letters and papers of Henry VIII, 1514.

Source C: :Leland's Itinerary, 1540.

1 Put the dates in the blank spaces. After _____ there was very little left of the cathedral and the houses of the bishop and the canons. In _____ permission was given to knock down the castle as well. By _____ there were no houses standing, outside or inside Old Sarum.

2 Why were the cathedral, castle and houses knocked down?

Answer:

3 Where was some of the stone from Old Sarum taken?

Answer:

22   Old Sarum

Unit 7. Old Sarum under the spade and trowel (1909-1915)

In 1909 Lt Colonel Hawley excavated what was then described as 'the citadel' of Old Sarum. This is the part we now call the inner bailey. Being a military man Hawley organised the excavation in a very precise way and had a little railway constructed, complete with branch lines and points, to dump the hundreds of tons of earth which were excavated. In 1939 Hawley's excavation diaries were given to Salisbury museum. Here are some extracts from the diaries:

May 31st 1910. *"The causeway having subsided since work ceased last year will need repair before trucks can run safely over it . . . Heavy gale and rain from SW which was almost continuous so that only a little work was done at intervals and (the) men left after their dinner hour.*

The work in hand was at the E and W ends of long wall core S of Tower. Foxwell found a boy who will be paid 1 shilling per day as was done last year, out of the gate-money."

June 1st 1910. *"Six men with 2 trucks working at tower footing at W end getting out some chambers and buttresses which have been come upon there. Three men with 1 truck working a cutting for branch line on E of tower footing, where they are finding only rubbish. Two men and boy are on the spoil bank levelling debris and sorting out flints. Works' carpenter . . . putting up garden fence."*

July 2nd 1910. *"No 2 Garderobe pit again produced many interesting objects today. Several pieces of window glass, some in better condition than those of yesterday. There were many fragments of yellow glass, possible of wine glasses, but the pieces were so utterly rotten they could not be touched without crumbling. Scales of fish were noticed on one or two occasions but were not preservable . . . The finding of these garderobe pits has attracted a great number of visitors and our takings at the gate, if the interest is continued, will soon pay for the erection of a barrier fence."*

The railway constructed by Hawley for the removal of excavated soil, 1909

1 From the June 1 1910 entry, calculate how many men worked on the site. (The carpenter counts as one of the men).

Answer:

2 How do we know that the Old Sarum excavations were popular with visitors?

Answer:

3 In August 1914 a problem arose that soon led to the early closing down of the site. Study these entries for 1914 and, in a few lines, explain what was going on.

August 1st. *"Grave warlike news today. It is rumoured that the Germans have invaded Belgian territory".*

August 3rd. *"No work done today. Ultimatum to Germany to evacuate Belgium".*

August 4th. *"No work done today. No men turned up for work, probably owing to the excitement of the declaration of war with Germany".*

August 5th. *"Two men turned up. A little work was done at the East parallel walls of the big building".*

Answer

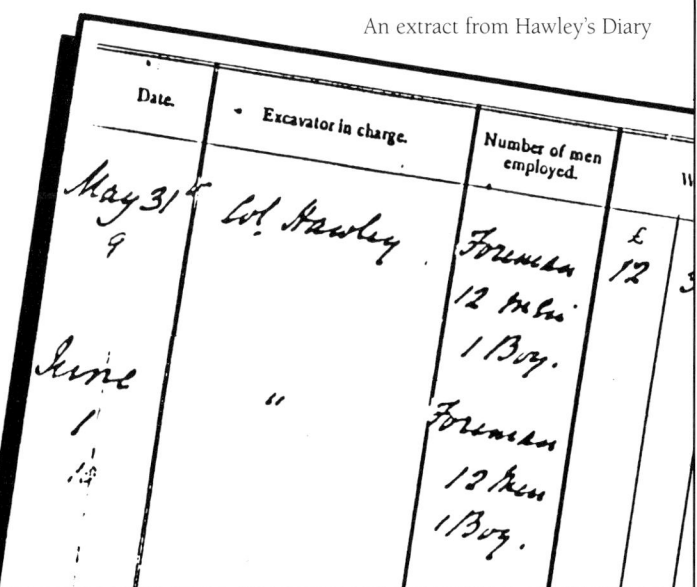

An extract from Hawley's Diary

Old Sarum

Unit 8. To excavate or not to excavate?

John Constable's watercolour painting of Old Sarum

"Nature had made it a sweet and beautiful spot; the earth over the old buried ruins was covered with an elastic turf, jewelled with the bright little flowers of the chalk...

Once only during the last five or six centuries some slight excavations were made when, in 1834, as a result of an excessively dry summer, the lines of the cathedral foundations were discernible on the surface. But it will no longer be the place it was, the Society of Antiquaries having received permission from the Dean and Chapter of Salisbury to work their sweet will on the site. That ancient beautiful carcass, which had long made their mouths water, on which they have now fallen like a pack of hungry hyenas to tear off the old hide of green turf and burrow down to open to the light or drag out the deep, stony framework. The beautiful surrounding thickets, too, must go, they tell me, since you cannot turn the hill inside out without destroying the trees and bushes that crown it."

Hudson, and others like him, would have preferred Old Sarum to be left as it was, wild and romantic, rather than have archaeologists excavate and find out more about Old Sarum and its history.

Divide into small groups. Decide whether you would have been on the side of Hudson or the archaeologists, and prepare a case for the view you have chosen. You may first need to consider what archaeologists find and how they work, and what they do with their finds.

Imagine there was a public hearing of these views. Elect a chairperson and ask people to speak from each point of view. Take a vote at the end to see which view was the most popular.

Photocopy and cut out for the vote! ▽

BALLOT PAPER

You may only vote for **ONE** point of view

Name: _____

FOR	**AGAINST**
Excavation on the Grounds of:	Excavation on the Grounds of:
☐ Mark with an **X**. Fold and place in Box	☐ Mark with an **X**. Fold and place in Box

Old Sarum

Name: .... Class: ....

Unit 9. The garderobe pits

The Norman part of Old Sarum was excavated between 1909 and 1915. The archaeologists found that most of the stone from Old Sarum had been taken away and had been used to build the new city of Salisbury. Only the foundations remained. Anything made of wood had, of course, rotted away and there were few Norman objects near the surface.

Then the excavators found the garderobe pits. These deep pits were where all the rubbish and sewage ended up. It had been too dangerous to remove the stone from the walls of these deep pits and they eventually filled up with rubble and earth from the crumbling ruins around them. The archaeologists found them very interesting. The excavation report says that:

"... in their haste to get the stone they (the stone robbers) buried the garderobe pits under the spoil created by breaking up the wall cores, extracting the facing stone and better masonry ... These garderobe pits ... having become buried, the later spoilators (robbers) may have been unaware of their existence".

Five pits were excavated. The pits would have been a major health hazard and must have attracted rats and flies in spite of their depth. The smell must have been appalling too. The archaeological report said:

"The state of things, taken from a sanitary point of view, must have been horrible, and it was necessary to throw quicklime occasionally into the pits, layers of which were frequently met with."

However horrible these pits may have been when they were in use, they provide a valuable source of information on Norman life at Old Sarum.

Study the Archaeologist's Report (see p. 16) and the information given above.

Pit south of the Postern Tower, 1911

1 What sorts of objects survived in the pits?

Answer:

2 Which finds tell us about people's eating habits? What were these eating habits? For example, were the people at Old Sarum vegetarians?

Answer:

3 How do we know that there was trade and contact between Old Sarum and the coast?

Answer:

4 What did people do about the smell that came from the garderobe pits?

Answer:

5 Are there any finds which may have been thrown away by accident? Can you think of another explanation?

Answer:

6 Which find suggests a sport which we would now regard as too cruel?

Answer:

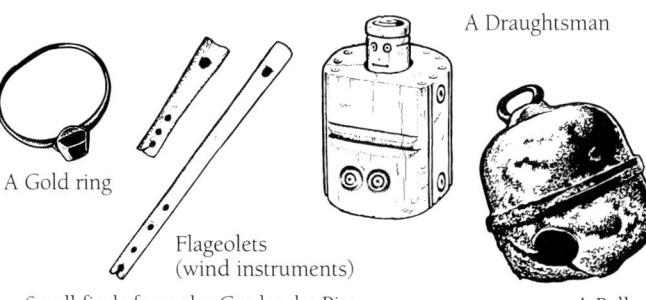

A Gold ring

Flageolets (wind instruments)

A Draughtsman

Small finds from the Garderobe Pits

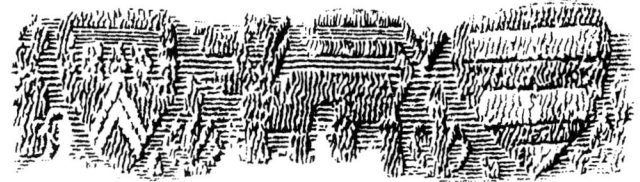

A Bell

A fragment of lace

Old Sarum

Name: .... Class: ....

Unit 10. Old Sarum and the modern landscape

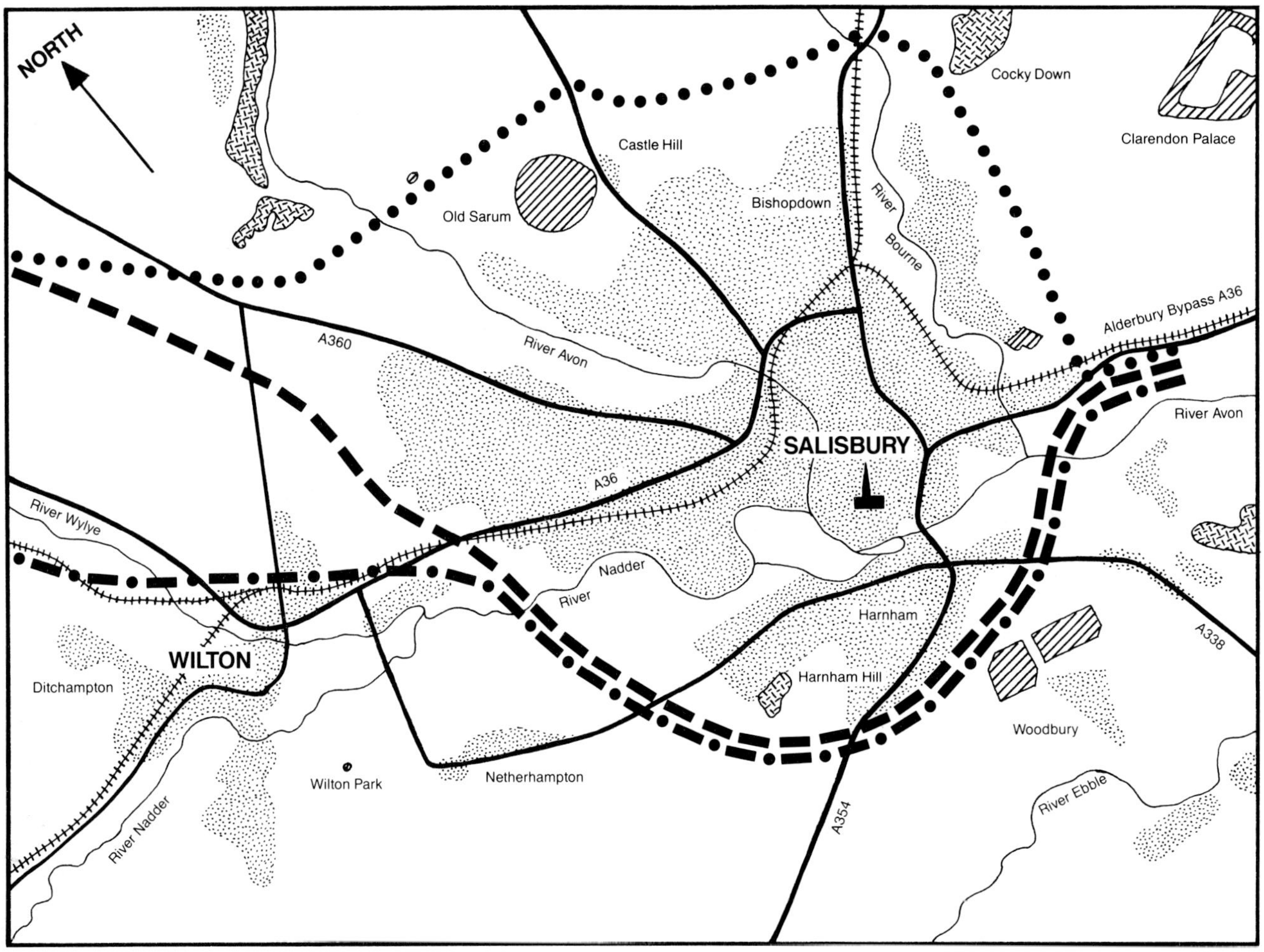

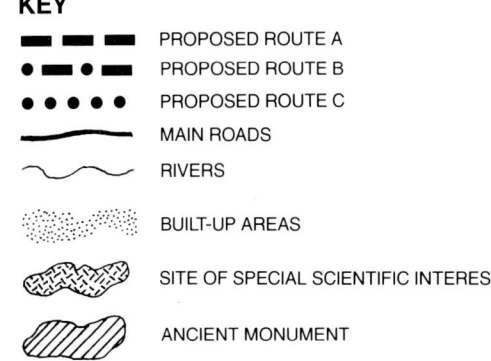

A map showing the three possible routes for a Salisbury by-pass

Look at the plan above. These are the three proposed routes for a much needed Salisbury by-pass. One route must be chosen, since Salisbury becomes more and more blocked by traffic.

Using your knowledge of Old Sarum, write a report on the case for or against routing the by-pass near Old Sarum, and made your own recommendations.

Report:

KEY

- ▬ ▬ ▬ PROPOSED ROUTE A
- ▬·▬·▬ PROPOSED ROUTE B
- ••••• PROPOSED ROUTE C
- ▬▬▬ MAIN ROADS
- ∼∼∼ RIVERS
- ░░░ BUILT-UP AREAS
- ▨▨▨ SITE OF SPECIAL SCIENTIFIC INTEREST
- ▨▨▨ ANCIENT MONUMENT
- ┼┼┼┼ RAILWAY LINES

Old Sarum

Visiting Old Sarum

An engraving of Old Sarum across a harvest field

A Guide To The Ruins

The visitor uses the east entrance to Old Sarum, the original Iron Age entrance to the hillfort and both the footpath and the road leading into the site have to circumvent the Iron Age hornwork in front of the East Gate.

Once inside the hillfort, which served as the outer bailey of the Norman castle, the inner bailey or 'citadel' as it is called in early maps, comes into sight. The outer bailey has never been excavated, and if it were to be excavated today, archaeologists would first have to remove the hundreds and hundreds of tonnes of earth tipped into this area by the excavators of 1909-1915.

Excavation would also prove beyond

It may not be immediately apparent what the remains at Old Sarum have to do with Old Sarum in the Iron Age, or Old Sarum in the Middle Ages. The visitor sees well trimmed grass, cemented foundations and the rubble core of old walls.

The site has gone through two millenia of development and even in the last hundred years there have been many changes.

The main problem the visit must tackle is the relationship between the very selective survival of periods of settlement and the scenes of vigorous animation, construction and everyday life that must have characterised events on this hill-top throughout the ages.

A visit requires an important and essential act of historical imagination, on the part of children, teachers and helpers to establish a relationship with the past.

One of the virtues of Old Sarum is that there is a great deal of space. It is also a site where children can be given a measure of freedom, with the strict proviso that they must neither climb on the walls nor down into the ditches.

An engraving of the East Gate

Visiting Old Sarum

doubt what most authorities now agree on, namely that the civil borough of Old Sarum was never within the Iron Age defences.

As we enter the inner bailey over the modern bridge, the foundations of the medieval bridges can be seen immediately below. It is only the foundations that were protected by the mass of rubble that accumulated on the site as the good building stone was removed by the builders of medieval Salisbury. This is why Hawley had to clear so many tonnes of material to expose what we can now so clearly see.

What Old Sarum lacks in architectural features, it makes up for in atmosphere, and it is as well to soak up the surroundings and orientate oneself before attempting a detailed examination of the site.

On The Day

Before settling down to fieldwork the following itinerary is recommended for the whole party, so that all concerned get an idea of the layout and extent of the site.

1. Head for the ramparts of the inner bailey, pausing only to explain entry through Iron Age defences, and entrance into Norman inner bailey.

2. Point out the following:
a. Modern Salisbury, dominated by cathedral
b. The foundations of the cathedral in the outer bailey
c. Salisbury plain to the north
d. The river Avon below Old Sarum
e. Clearbury Ring, another Iron Age Hillfort, visible to the south
f. The Roman roads.

3. Move into the inner bailey, the main features of which are:
a. **The Gatehouse** — two drum towers and a guard room on each side, at one time surmounted by a chamber and tower.
b. **Bishop Roger's Palace** — a large range of buildings halfway across the open space in the middle of the inner bailey and to the right. The palace was on at least two levels and the inner courtyard can clearly be distinguished on an upper level. The east and south wings were on a lower level and included a chapel. Several features survive, such as the departure of a staircase and a fireplace. The term 'palace' is really appropriate for this range of buildings, with only the tower, 'Bishop Roger's tower', north of the north-east corner, fulfilling a military function.

4. **The Postern Tower** — this massive building once stood next to the west, or 'postern', entrance to Old Sarum. The construction dates from the late 12th century, after Bishop Roger's disgrace and death. The quality and strength of this keep can be seen in some building stone which still survives in a distinctive series of battered, or slanted, courses. The keep contains an enormous garderobe pit, which can be inspected from above and whose lining, since it has been completely protected by rubble for several hundred years, gives an idea of the quality of the original stonework. There are several garderobe pits at Old Sarum, rubbish disposal must have been a constant problem.

A view of the footings of the early bridge, with an inset of Hawley, 1914

It is important to note that none of the rubble core which is the main feature of the site today was visible when Old Sarum was in use. All of this would have been covered in fine facing stone. The core was no more than a filler, as the inner walls were also faced.

Recently a section of wall on the ramparts immediately adjacent to the East Gate of the inner bailey has been exposed. This has been treated in such a way as to resemble the rubble core as exposed by excavation. This is a much more appropriate treatment than the earlier method applied to the rubble core on the rest of the site, where cement-based mortar is very much in evidence.

The two distinct cathedral plans are identified by two different types of surface. The effect of this is best observed from the rampart of the inner bailey.

Site Activity Sheet 1 The Inner Bailey of the Castle

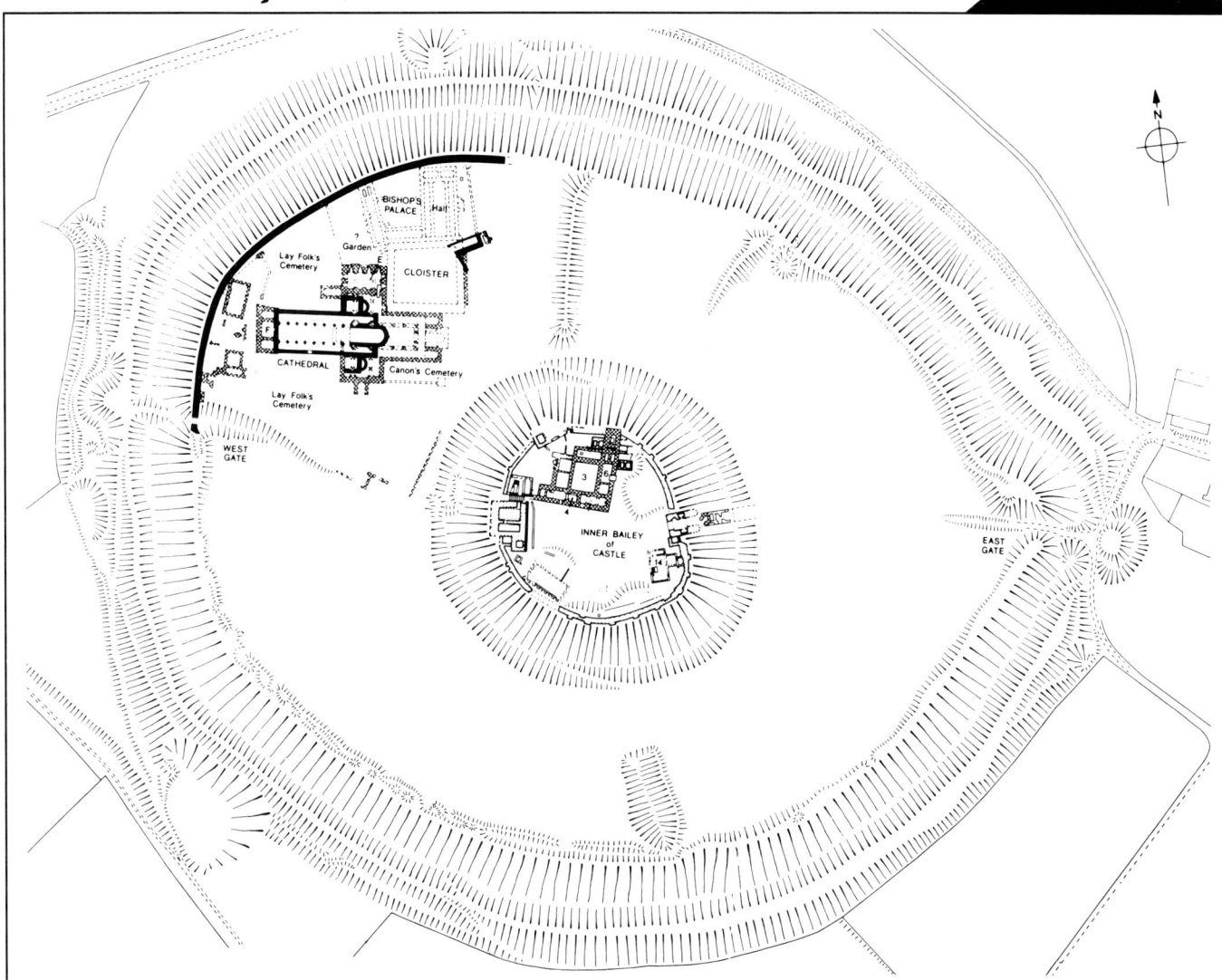

For this set of tasks you will need to use the plan of Old Sarum. Be prepared to do some walking but do not climb on the walls and on no account go down into the ditch of the outer rampart. You will also need to know where you are, which direction you are facing and which way the plan is facing. Make sure you have sorted this out before you start answering the questions.

Task 1
Under one bridge you will find the ruins of another. Find it, and mark it with the number '1' on your plan.

Task 2
What is the name of the first building you pass when entering the castle?

It is called:
Mark it with the number '2' on your plan.

Task 3
Go to the place marked '3' on your plan. You will find a grassy mound that was once a building.
What was this building?

It was:

What remains of this building above ground?
All that remains of this building is/are:

Task 4
What is marked '4' on your plan?

It is:

Why do you think this caused arguments between the bishop and the soldiers?

Answer:

Task 5
There was another entrance to the inner bailey. Where was it? When you have found it, mark it with the number '5' on your plan. What was this entrance called?

It was called the:

Old Sarum

Site Activity Sheet 2 The Outer Bailey

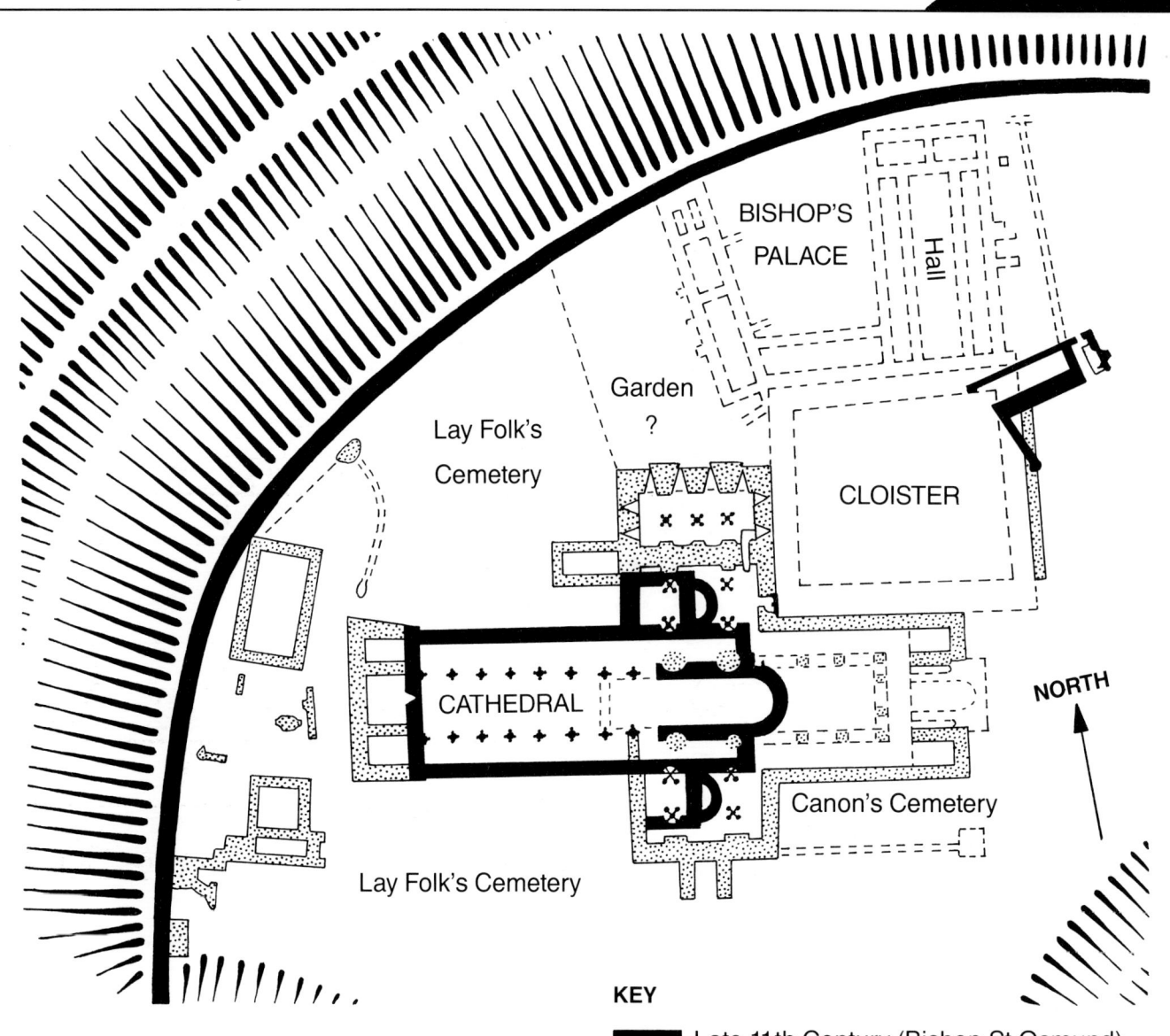

KEY

▇ Late 11th Century (Bishop St Osmund)

▒ Early 12th Century (Bishop Roger)

Explore the foundations of the cathedral in the outer bailey. Make sure you understand where the two cathedrals lay. One is much larger than the other.

Task Pace out the length of each cathedral. Try to use normal steps as you walk.

St Osmund's cathedral measures .... paces.

Bishop Roger's cathedral measures .... paces.

Before you leave Old Sarum have a good look round. Make any extra notes or sketches which will add interest to your work.

Is there anything which particularly interests you or anything important you have discovered?

(When you are visiting Salisbury museum in the cathedral close you may have time to pace out the length of the new cathedral by walking down the outside of the longest side. Compare this measurement with the length of the two cathedrals at Old Sarum.)

Notes/Sketch:

Site Activity Sheet 3 Looking at Stonework

Look at the illustration showing a typical section of wall at Old Sarum soon after most of the good building stone had been removed. Choose a section of wall that is similar to the illustration and then:

Task 1 — Shade the illustration to show the different types of building material.

Task 2 — Clearly fill in the labels provided, showing which is:

— Good building stone

— Rubble

— Flint and Mortar

Old Sarum

Site Activity Sheet 4 The Landscape of Old Sarum

Study sources 1 and 2 carefully. The sources show two typical Wiltshire landscapes.

Source 1
Landscape change — the expansion of settlements and services together with the loss of riverside vegetation and wet pasture by drainage works will gradually reduce their secluded qualities.

Source 2
Landscape change — a continued military presence with their requirements for development and training, including woodlands, will continue to be the greatest influence on landscape appearance.

1 Landscape subject Plan

Chalk River Valleys: meandering river, water meadows, secluded villages, dense tree cover and open chalk valley sides.

2 Landscape subject Plan

Salisbury Plain Plateau: gently undulating plain with extensive M.O.D. development.

1 In which direction do you see a landscape fitting the description in source 1?

Answer:

2 In which direction do you see a landscape fitting the description in source 2?

Answer:

3 Can you see any evidence in either landscape that echoes the landscape change forecast made a few years ago?

Answer:

Site Activity Sheet 5 Undercroft

Task 1 Go into the area marked 6 on your plan. You will see this pile of stones at one end of the room.

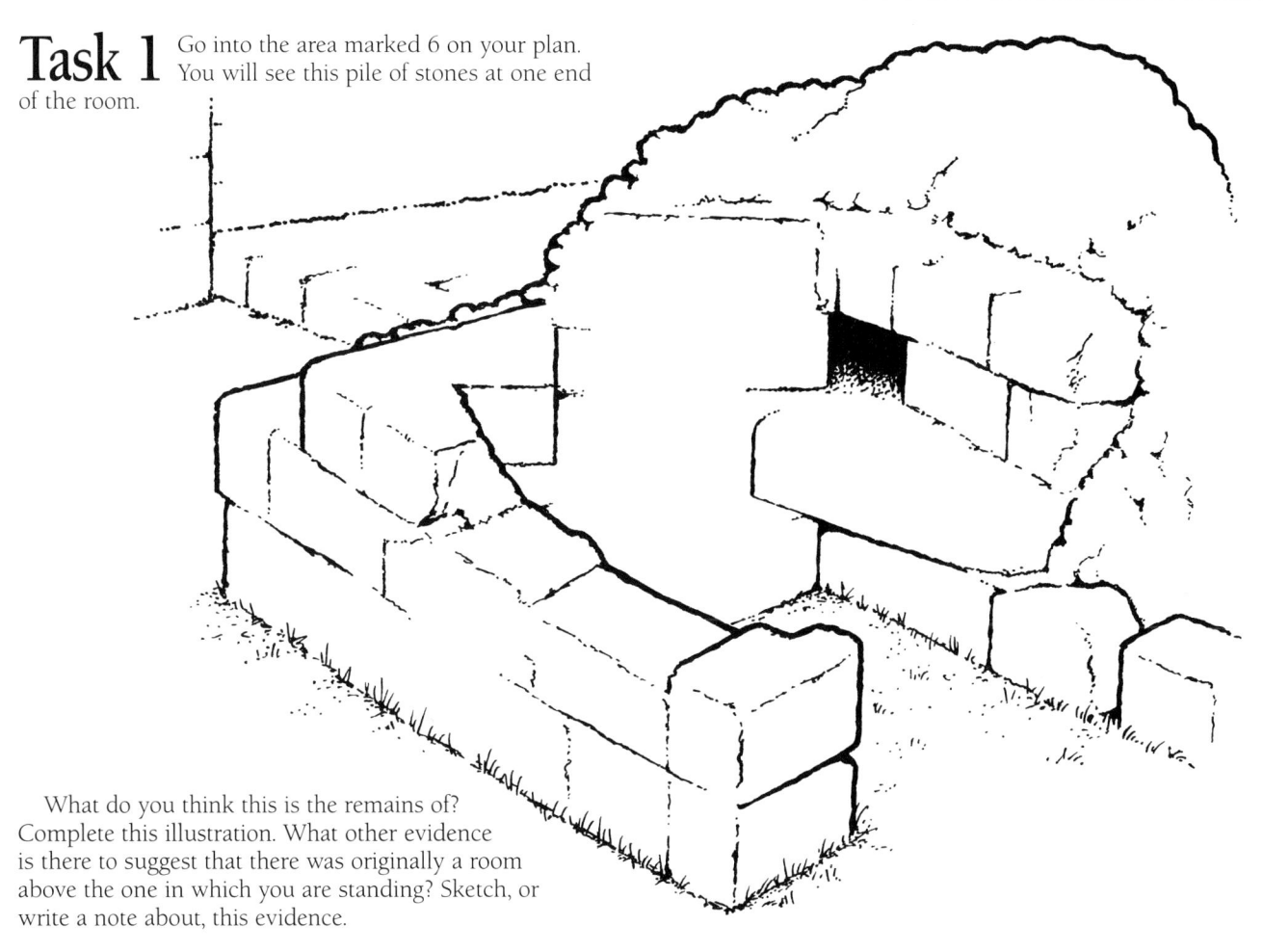

What do you think this is the remains of? Complete this illustration. What other evidence is there to suggest that there was originally a room above the one in which you are standing? Sketch, or write a note about, this evidence.

Sketch/note:

Why do you think this good quality stone was left behind when all the rest was removed for re-use elsewhere?

Answer:

Task 2 There are some parts of the wall that are still faced with good building stone. Make a rough sketch plan of the room. Mark these areas on your plan.

Plan:

Task 3 Sometime after this room was built a fire place was added half way along one of the walls. What evidence is there for the fireplace now?

Answer:

Old Sarum

Follow up work

How do Archaeologists and Historians Work?

1. 1. From what you know about Old Sarum complete the two following sentences:

a. An archaeologist gets his/her information from

b. A historian gets his/her information from

As we go further back in time there are fewer and fewer documents that survive. This is because documents get lost or destroyed and also, as we go further and further back, so fewer and fewer people knew how to write. When we get as far back as the early Iron Age, we come to a time when no one in England knew how to write.

WILL SURVIVE	WON'T SURVIVE

2. Very little is written down about Norman Old Sarum. What sort of things has archaeological excavation been able to tell us about Norman life at Old Sarum that we would not otherwise know?

Answer:

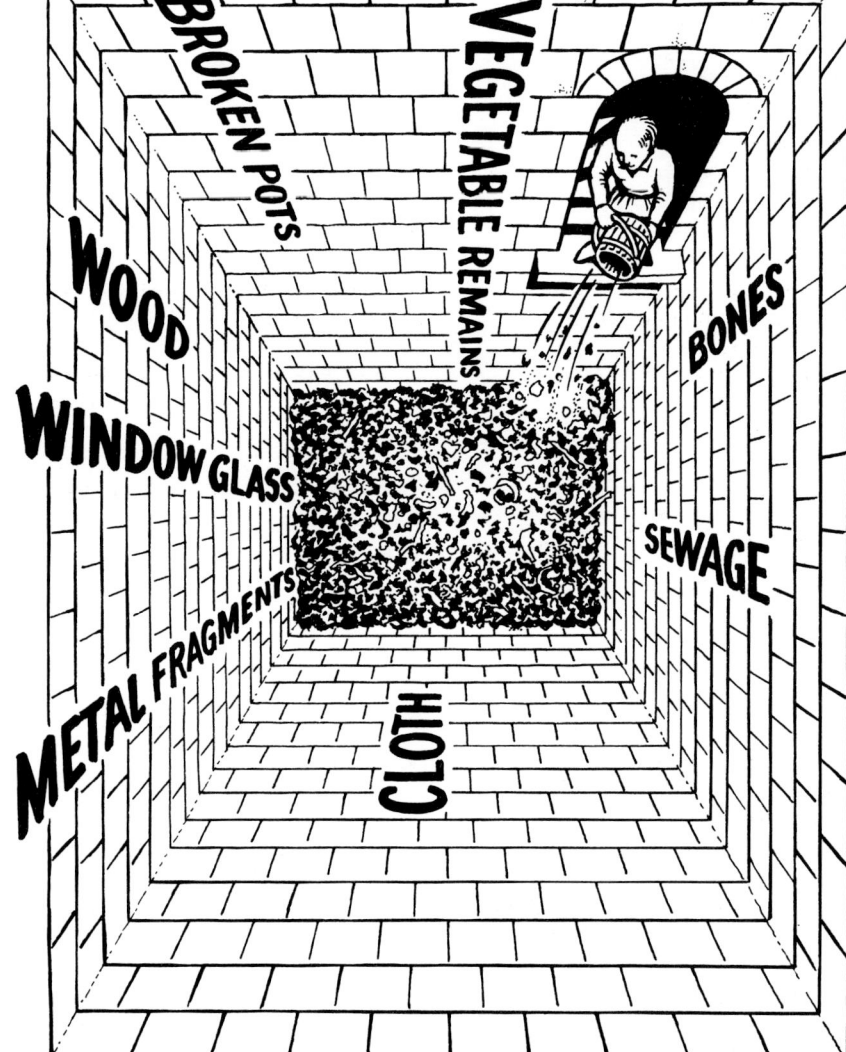

3. Some things just don't survive in the ground, they just rot or decay. Look at the illustration opposite and then in the two columns, 'will survive' and 'won't survive', put all the items you can see mentioned in the illustration in one or other of the two columns.

Old Sarum

Bibliography and Other resources

Bibliography

Books for Teachers

Unpublished Material

Old Sarum excavation diaries, 1910-1914, Lt Col Hawley, Salisbury Museum. Letter from General Pitt Rivers, Salisbury Museum.

A Shepherd's Life, W H Hudson, (1936 edition).
Calendar of Patent Rolls
Castles, a History and Guide, R Allen Brown, New Orchard Edition, 1980, ISBN 1 85078 013 2. Beautifully illustrated and wide ranging.
Endless Street, J Chandler, Hobnob Press, 1983, ISBN 0 94641 800 4.
Excavations at Old Sarum 1911-1916, Proceedings of the Society of Antiquaries.
Landscape Subject Plan, Wiltshire County Council, 1981.
Leland's Itinerary, Toulmin Smith (ed), 1906.
Letters and Papers of Henry VIII
Medieval England, Colin Platt, Routledge & Kegan Paul, 1978, ISBN 0 71008 815 9.
Old Sarum, H de S Shortt, HMSO Guide, 1965.
Poem on removal of Salisbury Cathedral, R Torrence, Wiltshire Archaeological Magazine, 1959.
The Medieval Builder, F Andrews, E P 1976. ISBN 0 85409 962 X — detailed study of different building crafts and individual craftsmen.
The Victoria History of Wiltshire VI, 1962.

Books for Children

Castle Life, Althea, Cambridge University Press, 1977, ISBN 0 52127 155 7. For younger children.
Castles, David Macaulay, Collins, 1977, ISBN 0 00195 128 9. A brilliantly illustrated story of a Welsh castle.
Growing Up in the Middle Ages, Penelope Davies, Wayland, 1972, ISBN 0 85340 174 8.
Looking at a Castle, Brian Davison, Kingfisher, 1987, ISBN 0 86272 251 9. Although written for the younger child, its illustrations are useful to older children.
The Middle Ages: Cultural Atlas for Young People, Mike Corbishley, Facts on File, 1990, ISBN 0 81601 973 8.

Fiction

Knight's Fee, Rosemary Sutcliff, Oxford University Press, 1974, ISBN 0 19277 066 7.
Siege of Swayne's Castle, R C Sherriff, Armada, 1975, ISBN 0 00671 056 5.
They Saw it Happen 55BC-1485AD, W O Hassall, Blackwell, 1959, ISBN 0 63105 280 1 — good extracts from original sources.

Archaeological Approaches

The Council for British Archaeology produces a series: *Archaeology for Schools*, (ISBN 0262 897X) of which *Upstanding Archaeology, Archaeology in the Classroom,* and *Archaeology in Primary Schools* are particularly useful. They are available from the CBA, 112 Kennington Road, London, SE11 6RE.

Drama and Role Play

Living History, Reconstructing the Past with Children, John Fairclough and Patrick Redsell, English Heritage, 1985, ISBN 1 85074 073 9.

Food and Cooking

Food and Cooking in Prehistoric Britain, Jane Renfrew, English Heritage, 1985, ISBN 1 85074 079 8.
Food and Cooking in Roman Britain, Jane Renfrew, English Heritage, 1985, ISBN 1 85074 080 1.
Food and Cooking in Medieval Britain, Maggie Black, English Heritage, 1985, ISBN 1 85074 081 1X.

These publications are available from English Heritage, PO Box 229, Northampton NN6 9RY.

English Heritage Videos

Available on free loan or purchase from English Heritage, PO Box 229, Northampton NN6 9RY.
Living History, for teacher training; 20 minutes; 1986.
Looking at a Castle, for age 11-13; 14 minutes; 1980.
The Norman Conquest for England, for aged 11-16; 15 minutes; 1982.

Slides and Software

Castles (A114): a set of 12 slides showing the development of castles.
Fletcher's Castle (Fernleaf). Castle building computer simulation.

Both distributed by the Slide Centre, Ilton, Ilminster, Somerset, TA19 9HS. Tel. 0460 57151.

Posters

A set of nine full colour photographic posters showing the development of castles and later fortifications can be purchased from English Heritage, PO Box 229, Northampton NN6 9RY.

Site Plan

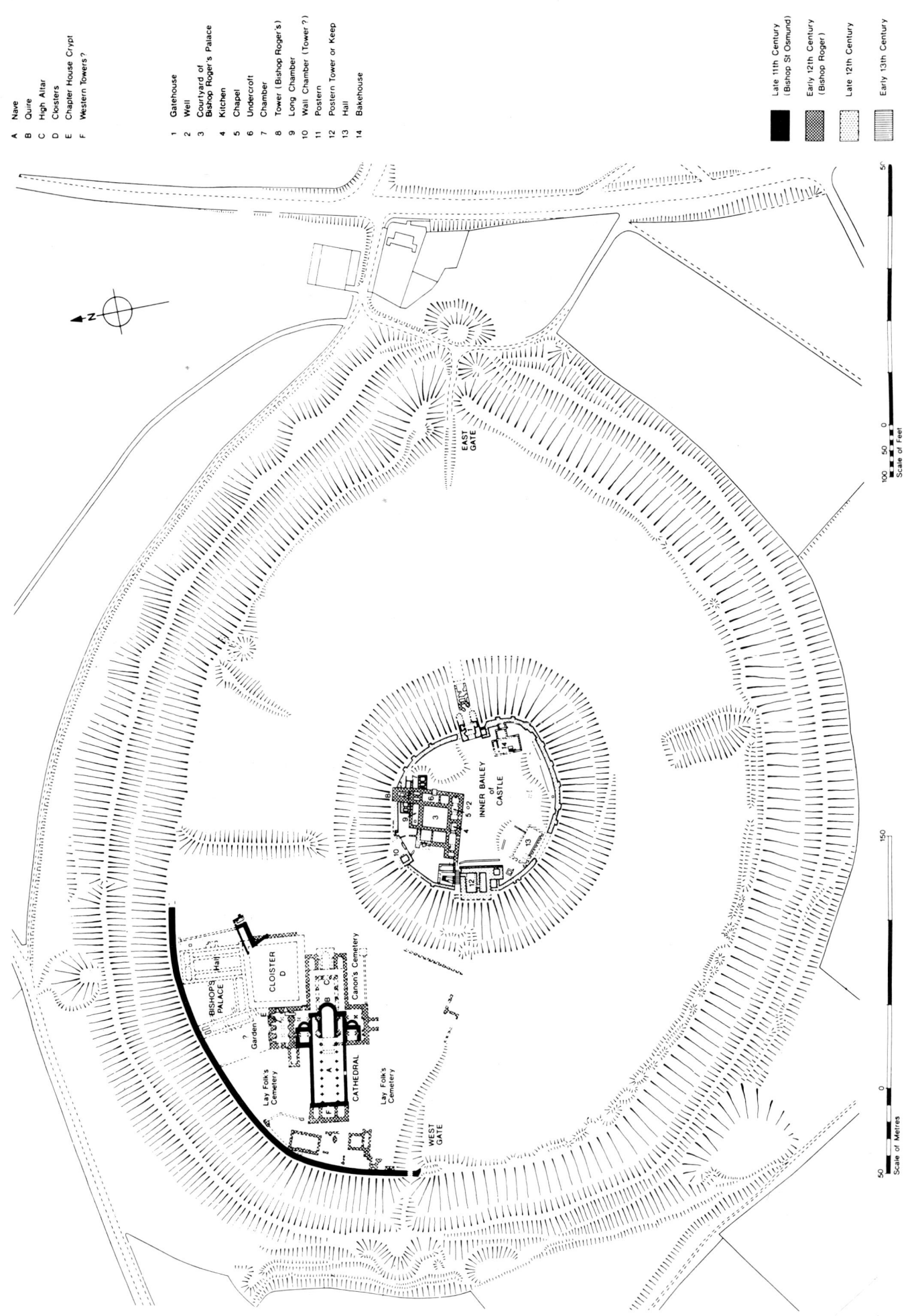

A Nave
B Quire
C High Altar
D Cloisters
E Chapter House Crypt
F Western Towers ?

1 Gatehouse
2 Well
3 Courtyard of Bishop Roger's Palace
4 Kitchen
5 Chapel
6 Undercroft
7 Chamber
8 Tower (Bishop Roger's)
9 Long Chamber
10 Wall Chamber (Tower ?)
11 Postern
12 Postern Tower or Keep
13 Hall
14 Bakehouse

■ Late 11th Century (Bishop St Osmund)
▦ Early 12th Century (Bishop Roger)
▨ Late 12th Century
▤ Early 13th Century